Lerner SPORTS™

ALL-STAR SMACKDOWN

CHRISTIAN PULISIC VS. CLINT DEMPSEY

WHO WOULD WIN?

LISA IDZIKOWSKI

Lerner Publications ◆ Minneapolis

For my family

Copyright © 2026 by Lerner Publishing Group, Inc.

All rights reserved. International copyright secured. No part of this book may be reproduced, stored in a retrieval system, or transmitted in any form or by any means—electronic, mechanical, photocopying, recording, or otherwise—without the prior written permission of Lerner Publishing Group, Inc., except for the inclusion of brief quotations in an acknowledged review.

Lerner Publications Company
An imprint of Lerner Publishing Group, Inc.
241 First Avenue North
Minneapolis, MN 55401 USA

For reading levels and more information, look up this title at www.lernerbooks.com.

Main body text set in Aptifer Sans LT Pro. Typeface provided by Linotype AG.

Editor: Anne E. Hill **Lerner team:** Sue Marquis

Library of Congress Cataloging-in-Publication Data

Names: Idzikowski, Lisa, author.
Title: Christian Pulisic vs. Clint Dempsey : who would win? / Lisa Idzikowski.
Description: Minneapolis : Lerner Publications, 2026. | Series: All-star smackdown (Lerner sports) | Includes bibliographical references and index. | Audience: Ages 7–11 | Audience: Grades 2–3 | Summary: "US soccer is rising, and striker Christian Pulisic is leading the way. But the path to success was paved by legendary players such as Clint Dempsey. Explore their careers and choose your soccer superstar"— Provided by publisher.
Identifiers: LCCN 2024038556 (print) | LCCN 2024038557 (ebook) | ISBN 9798765668528 (library binding) | ISBN 9798765683453 (paperback) | ISBN 9798765676011 (epub)
Subjects: LCSH: Soccer players—United States—Biography—Juvenile literature. | Pulisic, Christian, 1998-—Juvenile literature. | Dempsey, Clint, 1983-—Juvenile literature. | Soccer—United States—Juvenile literature.
Classification: LCC GV942.7.A1 I395 2026 (print) | LCC GV942.7.A1 (ebook) | DDC 796.334092/2—dc23/eng/20241009

LC record available at https://lccn.loc.gov/2024038556
LC ebook record available at https://lccn.loc.gov/2024038557

Manufactured in the United States of America
1-1011546-53820-11/21/2024

TABLE OF CONTENTS

Clint Dempsey

INTRODUCTION

SOCCER GREATS

In 2014, US Men's National Team (USMNT) star player Clint Dempsey made history. It was a hot, cloudy night in Brazil, and Dempsey was on fire. As captain, Dempsey quickly scored against Ghana.

 **Fast Facts** 

- Clint Dempsey scored 57 career goals with the USMNT.
- Dempsey is the only American male player to score in three World Cup games.
- Christian Pulisic is the only American man to play in and win a Union of European Football Associations (UEFA) Champions League game.
- Pulisic was named US Soccer Male Player of the Year four times.

Dempsey's goal became the US's fastest in a World Cup match. It was also the fifth fastest in tournament history. The US won the match 2–1. Dempsey played despite breaking his nose when he ran into another player during the game.

Seven years later, on April 27, 2021, the USMNT's Christian Pulisic also had a huge day. At only 22, he became the highest-scoring American player in UEFA Champions League history. Pulisic was the first American and youngest Chelsea Football Club player to score in a Champions League semifinal game.

Pulisic and his club from London, England, battled a tough rival in the semifinals. Chelsea had to beat Real Madrid to remain

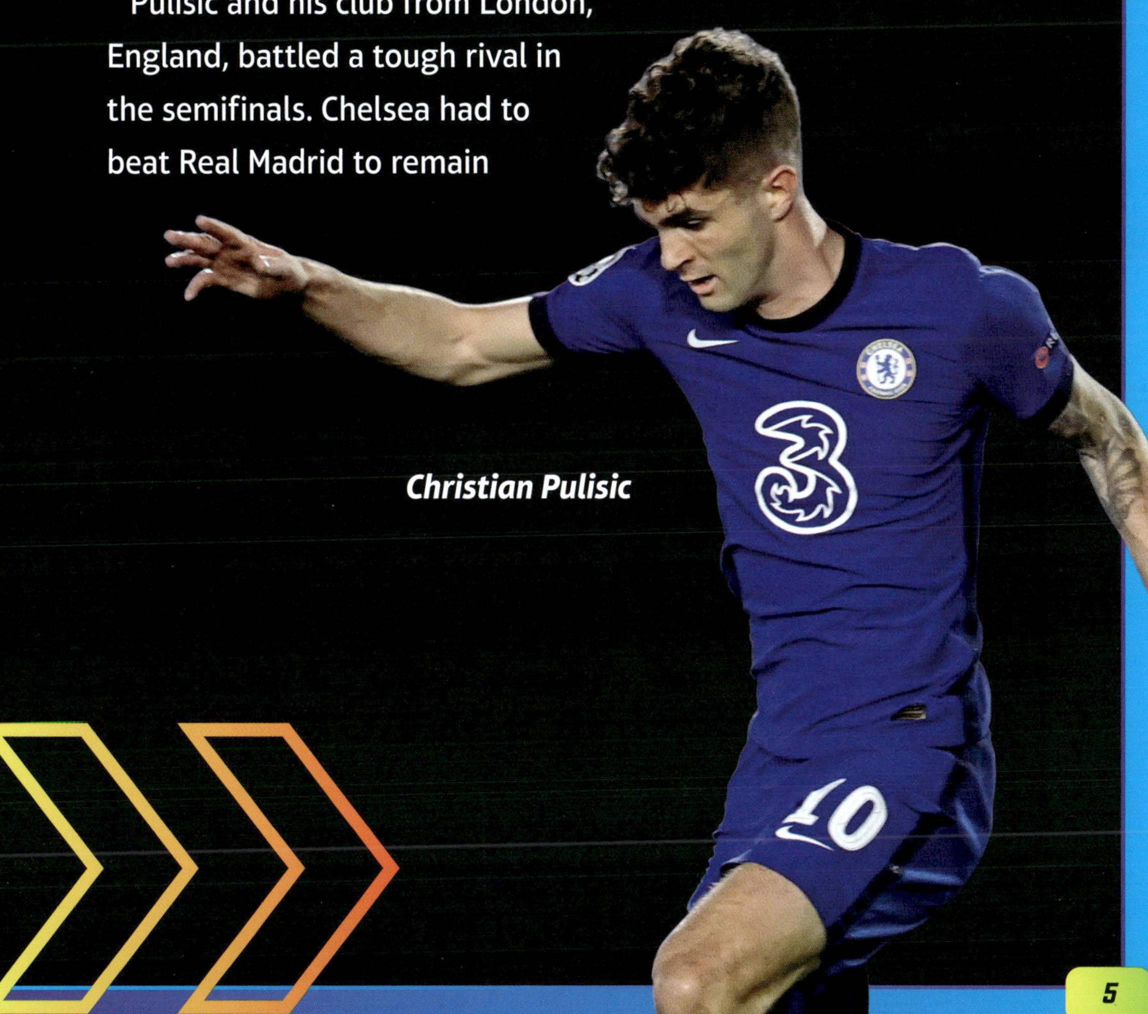

Christian Pulisic

in the UEFA tournament. Pulisic netted his big record-breaking goal 14 minutes into the game.

A teammate lofted the ball in his direction. Pulisic kicked it and dashed by a defender. He dribbled past the goalie. Seconds later, Pulisic took the shot. The ball flew into the goal, putting Chelsea in the lead.

Christian Pulisic and Clint Dempsey are great soccer players. But who is the best? You make the call. Let the smackdown start!

Dempsey (left) scores the first US goal versus Brazil at a World Cup match on June 16, 2014.

Pulisic (right) dribbles past Real Madrid player Toni Kroos at a match in April 2021.

CHAPTER 1

Dempsey (center) gets past two players from Portugal during a World Cup game.

BEGINNINGS

Clinton (Clint) Drew Dempsey was born on March 9, 1983, in Nacogdoches, Texas. Clint grew up with his parents and four siblings in this small East Texas town. The family lived in a mobile home in Clint's grandparents' backyard.

Clint and his older brother played soccer with neighborhood kids. They kicked a basketball around a dirt field and used rolled-up socks for goalposts. Clint played other sports too, but he became hooked on soccer.

When Clint was in fifth grade, his parents started driving him six hours round trip to Dallas, Texas. He played with the Dallas Texans, a top youth travel team. A few years later, he became a star player for his high school team.

Dempsey (left) gets a handshake from his brother Brian during his 2022 induction into the National Soccer Hall of Fame.

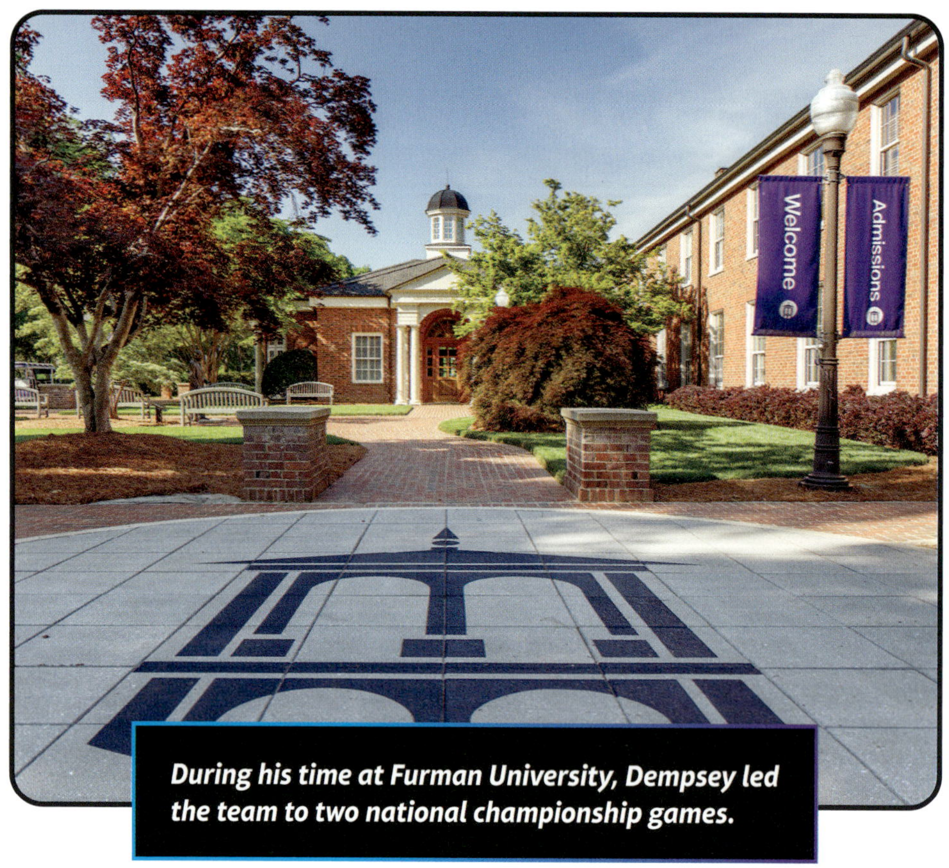

During his time at Furman University, Dempsey led the team to two national championship games.

In 2001, Dempsey's soccer career took off. He started playing at Furman University in South Carolina. In three years, he netted 17 goals and added 19 assists in 62 games. Dempsey led Furman to two national championship games.

At the 2004 Major League Soccer (MLS) draft, Dempsey went pro. He joined the New England Revolution. The USMNT also brought him on board. Playing for the Revolution, Dempsey was named MLS Rookie of the Year. He scored in the 2006 World Cup for the USMNT.

CONSIDER THIS

It's common for athletes to have nicknames. Christian Pulisic is called Captain America because of his amazing skills and leadership as captain of the USMNT. Clint Dempsey also has a nickname. People call him Deuce because he has worn the number 2 jersey since college. *Deuce* is another word for "two."

Christian Mate Pulisic was born on September 18, 1998, in Hershey, Pennsylvania. He and his older brother and sister grew up in a soccer family. His mom and dad had both played soccer in college. His dad later turned pro. By the time he could walk, Christian was watching his father play.

Pulisic (center) is joined by his parents, Mark (left) and Kelley, as he holds the UEFA Champions League trophy in 2021.

When he was six years old, Christian's family moved to England for a year. He joined a local youth soccer team called Brackley Town. He soon fell in love with the game, just as his parents had.

The Pulisic family moved back to Hershey. In 2008, Christian started playing with PA Classics, a team that was part of the US Soccer Development Academy. The academy trained promising young soccer players to become their best.

Pulisic grew up in the town of Hershey, Pennsylvania.

Pulisic (right) battles for the ball during a match in 2016.

Christian played many games with kids who were older and bigger than he was. In only four years, he joined the US Men's National Under-15 and then Under-17 teams. Coaches from the US and Europe took notice of him.

Christian's big break came in 2015. He moved to Germany and began training with a top German team. Within a year, he had turned pro. He began playing for the famous club Borussia Dortmund, also called BVB.

CHAPTER 2

Dempsey is lifted up by his teammates after a goal at the 2010 World Cup.

PERFECT PLAYS

Dempsey's pro career began after three years of playing college soccer at Furman University. He joined the New England Revolution in 2004. The Revolution picked him eighth in the MLS draft that year. In three seasons with the team, he scored 25 goals in 71 games. Dempsey also played for the USMNT. In 2006, he scored the team's only goal in the World Cup.

In England's Premier League, Dempsey played for the club team Fulham. He became a top European player. In a 2012 match, 28-year-old Dempsey sizzled. He found the net three times in only 30 minutes. First, he scored a goal from three yards away.

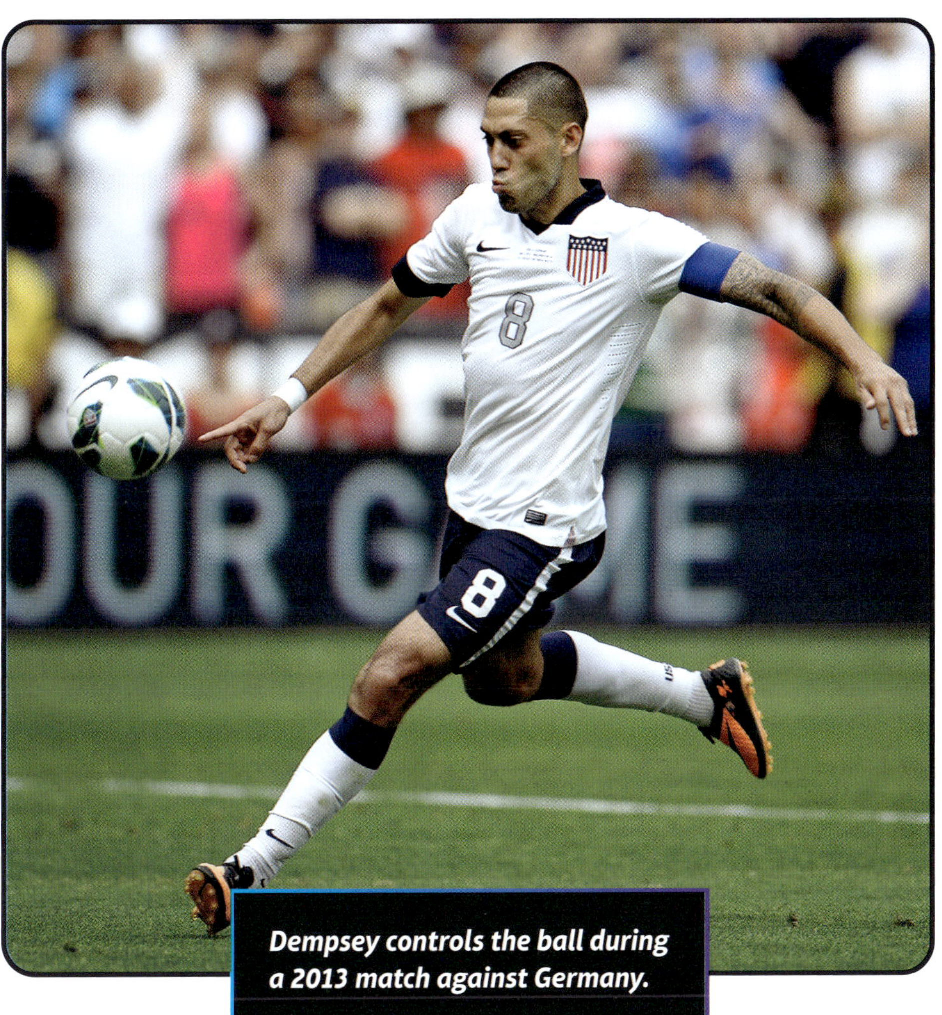

Dempsey controls the ball during a 2013 match against Germany.

Six minutes later, he booted one in from close range. About 20 minutes later, he scored his third goal. It was his first Premier League hat trick.

In June 2016, the USMNT star delivered again for his team. It was a tough game against Ecuador. The winner would go on to the semifinals in Copa America. Dempsey headed one into the net 22 minutes into the match. The US won 2–1.

While Dempsey was becoming a soccer star, Christian Pulisic moved to Germany and started training with BVB. Playing as a teenager on their U-19 team, he scored 10 goals in 15 matches. USMNT coaches started paying attention to the young player.

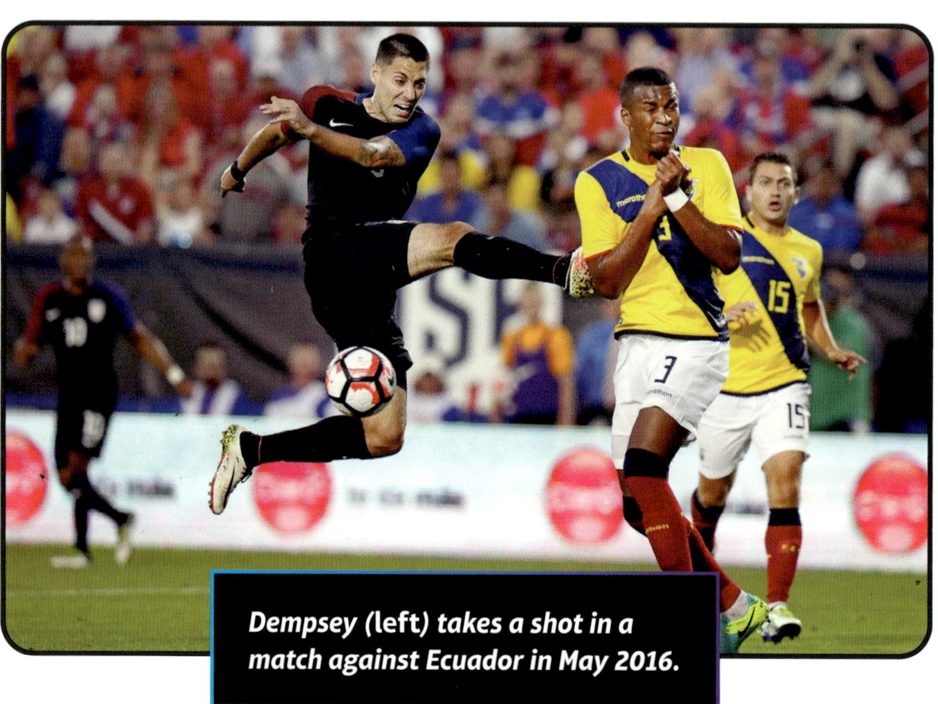

Dempsey (left) takes a shot in a match against Ecuador in May 2016.

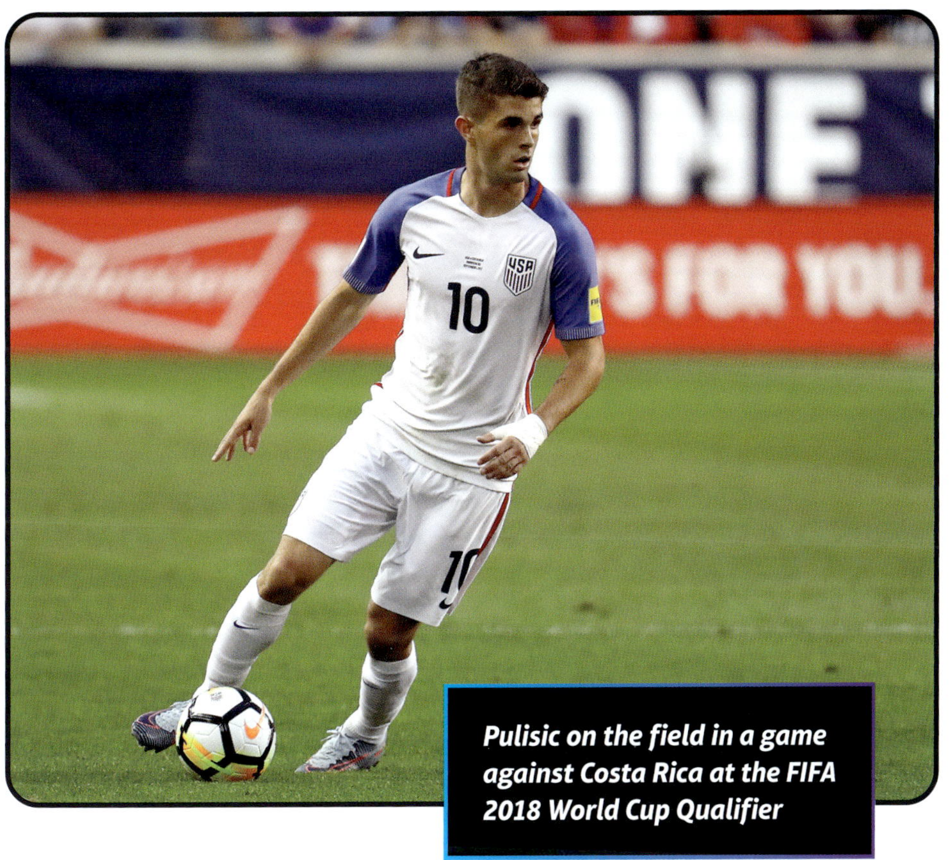

Pulisic on the field in a game against Costa Rica at the FIFA 2018 World Cup Qualifier

In March 2016, Christian played in his first US soccer match. He became the youngest man to play in a match to qualify for the World Cup. About a month later, Christian was back on the field for his German club.

In minute 38 of an exciting match against Hamburg, BVB's captain passed to Christian. Christian took the pass and blasted a low shot inside the near goalpost. With this goal, the 17-year-old US star became the youngest non-German player to ever score for the club.

CONSIDER THIS

In 2019, 20-year-old Pulisic became the most expensive American soccer player of all time. Chelsea Football Club paid nearly $73 million to transfer him to their team.

Pulisic had always wanted to play in the Premier League. After 90 matches and 13 goals for BVB, he joined the Premier League's Chelsea Football Club. In October 2019, Pulisic scored a hat trick for Chelsea. This made him the second American to do this in the Premier League. Dempsey was the first.

Pulisic scores the first goal for Chelsea in a match versus Manchester City on June 25, 2020.

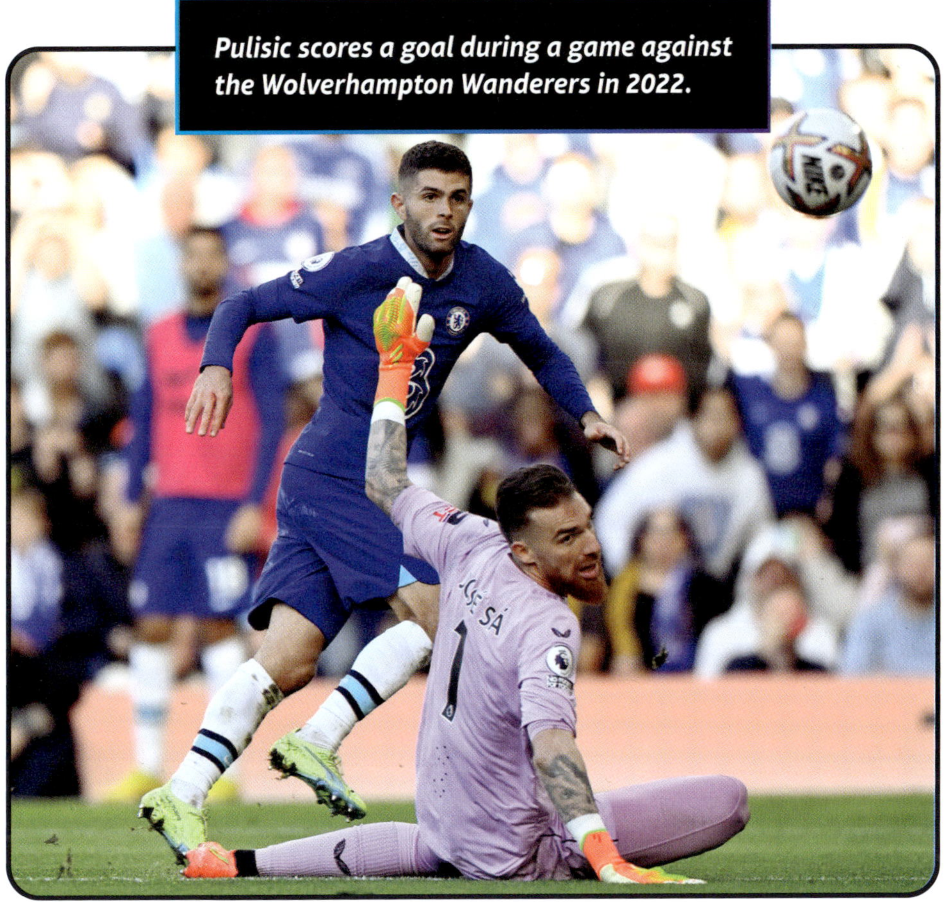

Pulisic scores a goal during a game against the Wolverhampton Wanderers in 2022.

Pulisic also continued playing for the USMNT. He had two goals in a Confederation of North, Central America and Caribbean Association Football (CONCACAF) game in the summer of 2023. The goals set up a 3–0 win against Mexico.

The following spring, Pulisic played for both the USMNT and Italian club AC Milan. He became the first Milan midfielder to shoot the ball on the net more than 10 times in a season since 2006. He helped end the team's six-match losing streak.

CHAPTER 3

Dempsey gives a thumbs up after scoring three goals at the Gold Cup Quarterfinal in 2015.

AWESOME AWARDS

Pulisic and Dempsey are two of soccer's most awarded players. They have had successful careers with the USMNT and their club teams. Pulisic is ranked the fifth-best-scoring player for the USMNT with 30 goals. Dempsey is tied for first place with 57. Both men have been captains for the USMNT.

Dempsey played nine seasons in MLS. He was MLS Rookie of the Year in 2004. He was also an MLS All-Star in 2005, 2006,

2014, and 2015. Dempsey earned USSF Soccer Player of the Year titles in 2007, 2011, and 2012.

Neither Pulisic nor Dempsey has won a World Cup. But Dempsey has played in (and scored in) three World Cups. This made him the first American player to score in three different World Cups. Dempsey first became captain of the team in 2013. He was the captain in the 2014 World Cup.

Dempsey dribbles down the field during a match against Costa Rica on March 22, 2013.

CONSIDER THIS

Dempsey enjoys hunting, fishing, and golf. Since retiring from playing soccer, he has worked as a TV sports broadcaster for CBS and FOX Sports.

Pulisic first wore the captain's armband in November 2018. At 20, he was the youngest captain for the USMNT since 1990. Pulisic was named USSF Soccer Player of the Year in 2017, 2019, 2021, and 2023. That puts him in a tie with another USMNT great, Landon Donovan. Pulisic was named CONCACAF Nations League Best Player in the 2023 tournament. The USMNT has won the tournament three times with Pulisic as their captain.

Pulisic takes a shot on goal during the CONCACAF Gold Cup Quarterfinal in 2019.

Pulisic displays his player of the tournament trophy at the CONCACAF Nations League Final in 2023.

CHAPTER 4

Dempsey (left) scores a second goal during the FIFA 2018 World Cup Qualifier match in 2017.

AND THE WINNER IS

Who is the winner of this all-star soccer smackdown? Dempsey and Pulisic are two all-time great players. No answer is right or wrong. People will form their own opinions. That's what makes being a sports fan fun. Who do you think is the best player?

Dempsey and Pulisic have both played as forwards for the USMNT. They also have both been captains. They have both been standouts for their club teams.

During Dempsey's Team USA career, he netted 57 goals in 141 games. He's tied with Landon Donovan as the USMNT's leading scorer. Dempsey is also the first US player to score in three World Cup tournaments. He played in 10 World Cup matches and scored four total goals.

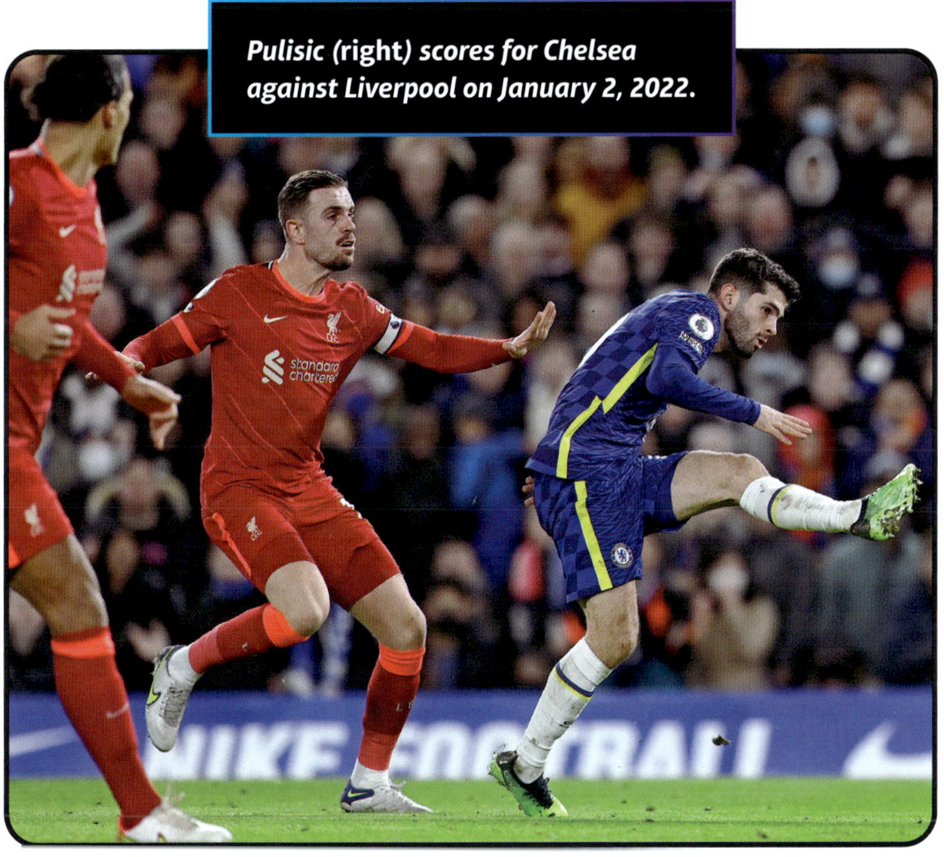

Pulisic (right) scores for Chelsea against Liverpool on January 2, 2022.

Dempsey earned the USSF Player of the Year award three times. He retired from playing soccer in August 2018. He joined the National Soccer Hall of Fame in 2022.

Pulisic first played for Team USA in 2016. During Pulisic's USMNT career, he has scored 30 goals in 71 games. He is currently the USMNT's sixth-leading scorer. He has scored once in four World Cup matches. Pulisic is the first American man to play in and win a UEFA Champions League game. He has been awarded USMNT Player of the Year four times.

It is hard to choose a winner. Both soccer stars have made exciting plays for their club and national teams. Pulisic has years left to play to beat Dempsey's impressive stats. But Dempsey wins this smackdown for now. Think it over, and make your own decision on the winner.

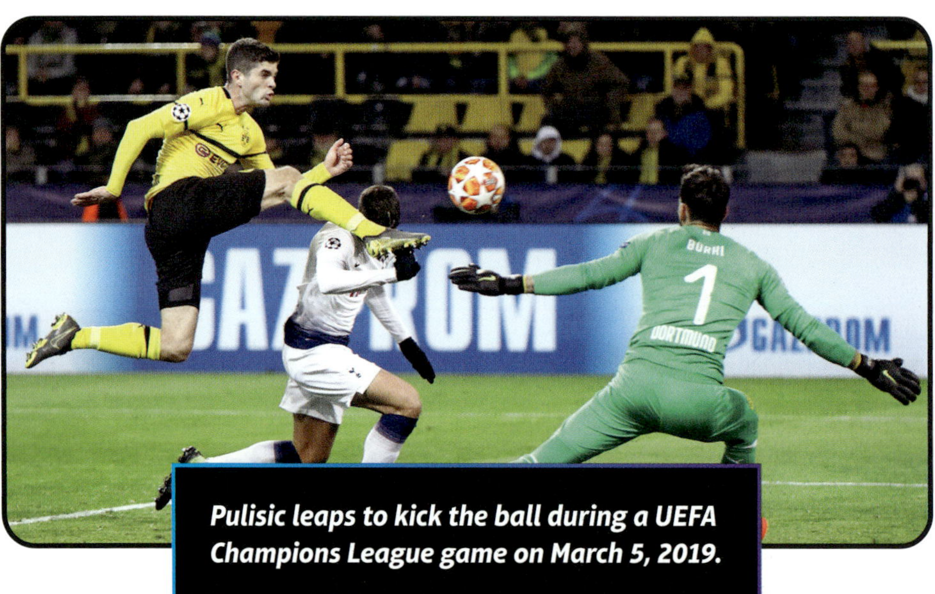

Pulisic leaps to kick the ball during a UEFA Champions League game on March 5, 2019.

Dempsey (left) fights for the ball in a World Cup Qualifier match against Honduras.

SMACKDOWN BREAKDOWN

CLINT DEMPSEY

Height: 6 feet 1 (1.8 m)
USMNT goals: 57
USMNT assists: 21
USSF Player of the Year awards: 3

Stats are accurate through the 2023 season.

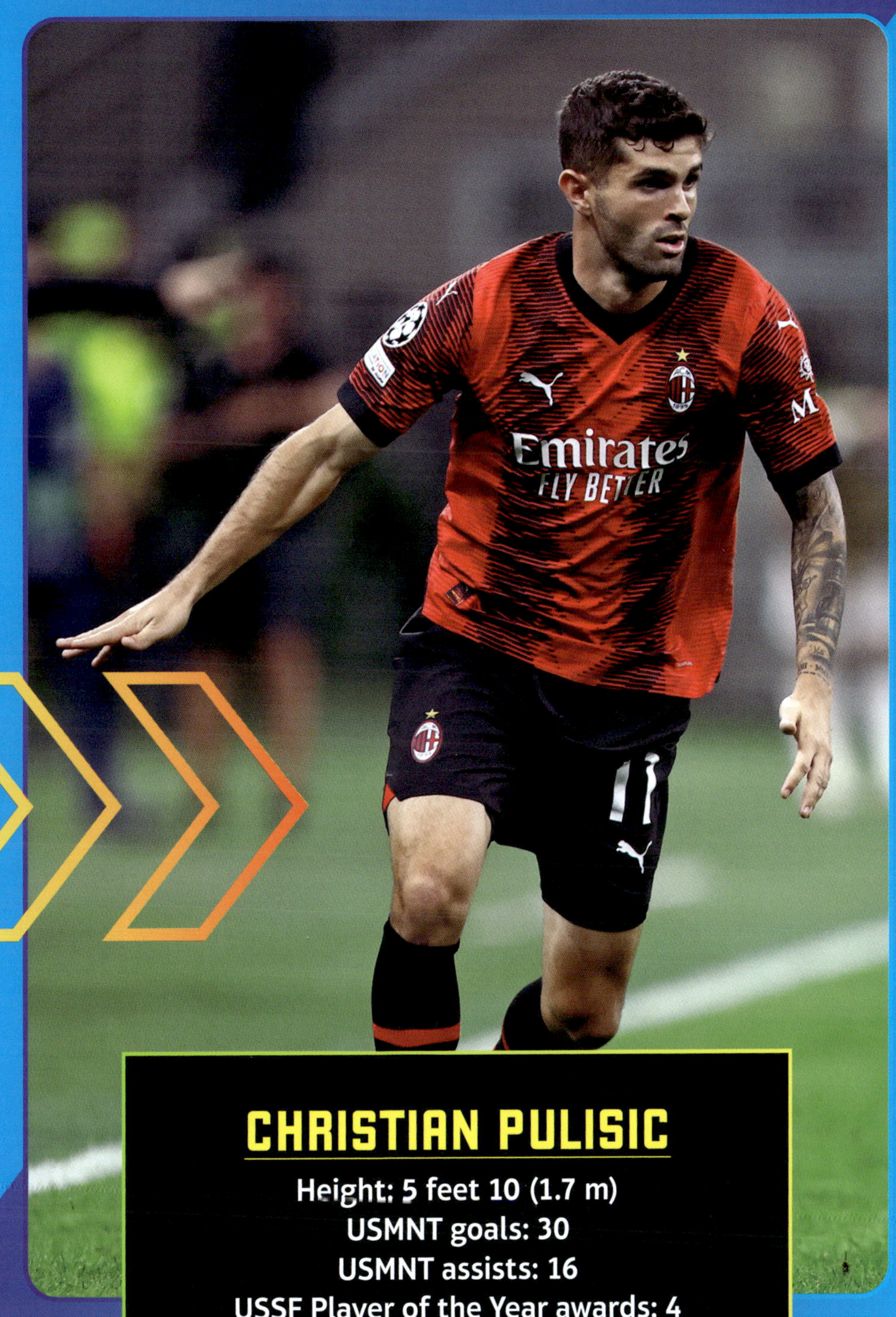

CHRISTIAN PULISIC

Height: 5 feet 10 (1.7 m)
USMNT goals: 30
USMNT assists: 16
USSF Player of the Year awards: 4

GLOSSARY

captain: a player who is the official leader of a team

club: a pro soccer team

dribble: to control the soccer ball with a player's feet

forward: a player whose main job is to score goals

hat trick: when a player scores three goals in one game

head: to hit and direct a soccer ball with your head

pro: short for *professional*, taking part in an activity to earn money

semifinal: a game or a series of games coming before the final round in a tournament

UEFA: a group that oversees soccer in Europe

LEARN MORE

Anderson, Josh. *Lionel Messi vs. Pelé: Who Would Win?* Minneapolis: Lerner Publications, 2024.

Gitlin, Marty. *Ticket to the FIFA World Cup*. Ann Arbor, MI: Cherry Lake, 2023.

Kiddle: Christian Pulisic Facts for Kids
https://kids.kiddle.co/Christian_Pulisic

Kiddle: Clint Dempsey Facts for Kids
https://kids.kiddle.co/Clint_Dempsey

Leed, Percy. *Pro Soccer by the Numbers*. Minneapolis: Lerner Publications, 2025.

Sports Illustrated Kids: Soccer
https://www.sikids.com/tag/soccer

INDEX

PHOTO ACKNOWLEDGMENTS

Image credits: Streeter Lecka/Getty Images, p. 4; Javier Soriano/AFP via Getty Images, p. 5; Michael Steele/Getty Images, p. 6; David S. Bustamante/Soccrates/Getty Images, p. 7; Dennis Grombkowski/FIFA via Getty Images, p. 8; Omar Vega/Getty Images, p. 9; BSPollard/Getty Images, p. 10; Darren Walsh/Chelsea FC via Getty Images, p. 11; Candy Delaney/Getty Images, p. 12; Guido Kirchner/picture alliance via Getty Images, p. 13; Kevork Djansezian/Getty Images, p. 14; Dennis Grombkowski/Bongarts/Getty Images, p. 15; Tom Pennington/Getty Images, p. 16; Mike Lawrie/Getty Images, p. 17; Julian Finney/Getty Images, p. 18; Justin Setterfield/Getty Images, p. 19; Matthew Ashton - AMA/Getty Images, pp. 20, 23; Dustin Bradford/Getty Images, p. 21; Ira L. Black/Corbis via Getty Images, p. 22; David Madison/Getty Images, pp. 24, 25; Alex Grimm/Bongarts/Getty Images, p. 26; Shaun Clark/Getty Images, p. 27; Kevin C. Cox/Getty Images, p. 28; sportinfoto/DeFodi Images via Getty Images, p. 29.

Cover images: Giuseppe Maffia/NurPhoto via AP Images (Pulisic); George Holland/Cal Sport Media via AP Images (Dempey).